CAMPING COOKBOOK

SIMPLE CAMPFIRE RECIPES FOR DUTCH OVEN, CAST IRON AND 5 MORE METHODS

Table of Contents

Introduction 10
Chapter 1: On a Stick 13
    Breakfast 15
        Sausage Biscuit with Pancake Syrup.............15
        Cheesy Biscuit on a Stick................................16
        Campfire Bacon 17
        Cinnamon Rollups...18
    Main Dish 19
        Steak on a Stick 19
        Hot Dogs on a Stick 20
    Side Dish 21
        Campfire Bread on a Stick 21
        Antipasto Stick for RV Campers....................23
    Dessert 24
        Shortcake on a Stick 24
        Apple Pie on a Stick 26
Chapter 2: Kebab on Skewers....................................28
    Breakfast 29
        French Toast Sausage Kebabs for RV Campers...29
        Savory Breakfast Kebabs...............................31
        Brown Breakfast Skewers 32
    Main Dish 34
        Chicken and Veggie Kebabs..........................34

- Beef and Onion Skewers 36
- Beef Kebab 37
- Vegan Kebabs 39
- Smoked Sausage Kebabs 41
- Dessert 42
  - Marshmallow and Strawberry Kebabs 42
- Chapter 3: Grate 43
  - Breakfast 45
    - Grilled French Toast 45
    - Cheese Sandwich 47
    - Grilled Breakfast Patties 48
  - Main Dish 49
    - Grilled Leg of a Lamb 49
    - Grilled Salmon 51
    - Herb Chicken Thighs 52
    - Grilled Beef-Mushroom Burgers 53
    - Grilled Chicken and Corn Quesadilla 55
  - Side Dish 57
    - Grilled Wings 57
    - Grilled Potatoes 59
  - Dessert 60
    - Grate-Grilled Marshmallows 60
    - Honey-Rum Grilled Bananas 61
- Chapter 4: Pie Iron 62
  - Breakfast 64

Breakfast Sandwich 64
Ham Omelet 66
Banana Nutella breakfast biscuits 67
Main Dish 68
Super Easy Chicken Pot Pie 68
Monte Cristo 70
Pie Iron Pizza 71
Pie Iron Chicken Pesto Wraps 72
Chicken Chimichangas 73
Dessert 74
Campfire Fruit Pies 74
Peanut Butter Banana Sandwich 75
Chapter 5: Dutch Oven 76
Breakfast 79
Mountain Man Breakfast Casserole 79
Sausage and Egg Breakfast 81
Breakfast Burritos 82
French Toast Casserole 84
Family Quiche 86
Main Dish 88
Dutch Oven Nachos 88
Sprite Chicken 90
Baked Beans 92
Dutch Oven Macaroni and Cheese 94
Dessert 95

Dutch Oven Perry Cobbler Pie 95
Caramel Apple Cobbler 97

Chapter 6: Cast Iron Skillet 98

Breakfast 100
Campfire Skillet Breakfast 100
Crustless Quiche 101
Cast Iron French Toast 102
Bacon Asparagus Frittata 103

Main Dish 105
Hot Mess 105
Potatoes with Parmesan 107
Cast Iron Skillet Vegetables 109
Simple Skillet Lunch/Dinner 110

Dessert 111
Berries, Chocolate, and Vanilla Skillet 111
Maple Syrup Pudding Cake 112

Chapter 7: Foil Packets 114

Breakfast 115
Egg Bake Breakfast 115
Foil Packet French Toast 116
Sandwich Loaf with Ham and Cheese 118

Main Dish 120
Indian Spiced Baked Potato in Foil 120
Country Potatoes 121
Shrimpy Steak Foil Packet 122

Foil Packaged Chicken Breast......................123

　　Lemon Garlic Foil Packet............................124

　　Jambalaya Foil Packet................................125

　　Bacon Ranch Chicken Packet.....................126

　　Easy Baked Fish in Foil Packets.................128

　Dessert...130

　　Banana Marshmallow in Foil Packet............130

Chapter 8: Camping Shopping List......................131

Conclusion...133

Introduction

Camping Cookbook is ideal for all campers who fully immerse themselves in the whole experience. Fresh air, stress relief, increased physical activity levels, better sleep, and better mood are just some of the many benefits of camping. It also happens to be the perfect opportunity to escape a hectic lifestyle and spend quality time with friends and family.

In order to make camping an unforgettable experience, we make sure to bring all the equipment and gear necessary, but what about food? Energy bars and other products bought in the store are not the solutions. Camping cooking is a fun experience, and the result is delicious food made without too much hassle. What makes camping cooking so amazing is that you can make tasty meals using a few ingredients only. It's a great way to spend some time outdoors and allows your mind and body to enjoy the scenery around you as well as the scent and taste of the food you have just prepared.

Campers have various cooking methods at their disposal, including a Dutch oven, pie iron, cast iron skillet, on a stick, kebab on skewers, grate, and more. This Camping Cookbook delivers a plethora of recipes for each cooking method. All meals from this cookbook are easy to prepare and require no culinary experience. Whether you're a cooking rookie or a pro, this Camping Cookbook will revolutionize the way you camp.

Easily accessible ingredients, simple recipes, multiple cooking methods, and delicious meals, in the end, make Camping Cookbook every camper's must-have. Go through the cookbook, choose the recipes you like the most, and get all the ingredients ready for your next camping trip.

Food brings people closer together and enhances the overall camping experience. Recipes from this cookbook can serve as a wonderful source of inspiration to develop your creativity and experiment with various cooking methods to come up with your own meals. All you need is willpower and imagination. Take your camping trips to a whole new level with this cookbook.

Chapter 1: On a Stick

Camping is all about simplicity, and cooking methods should be the same. Cooking on a stick is one of the easiest methods for campers. Why? The reason is simple, this style of preparing food requires almost no preparation, or a vast selection of tools and equipment, just a stick. Particularly useful cookbook for everyone who is camping in tents. Build a fire and find a stick nearby, and that's it. To make this cooking method more effective, you need a stick long enough to enable you to sit far enough from fire to avoid burning yourself. Of course, the stick should also be sturdy enough to avoid dropping the food in the flame. Options for cooking on a stick are endless; everything that fits and remains secure on the stick can be used for breakfast, lunch, or dinner when camping.

Breakfast

Sausage Biscuit with Pancake Syrup

INGREDIENTS FOR 1 SERVING

- Biscuit baking mix – 1 cup/200g
- Sugar – 1tbsp
- Milk – 1/3 cup
- Egg – 1
- Vanilla extract – ½ tsp
- Precooked smoked sausage ring – 1 package
- Maple syrup – to taste

COOKING TIME: 5 MINUTES

METHOD

- Combine baking mix, sugar, egg, and vanilla until well blended
- Cut the sausage into equal pieces and pierce a stick through it
- Dip sausage in the biscuit batter and coat thoroughly
- Cook over the fire for 10 minutes or until the biscuit turns golden brown
- Serve with maple syrup

Cheesy Biscuit on a Stick

INGREDIENTS FOR 6 SERVINGS

- Baking mix – 17.6oz/500g package
- Water – ½ cup
- Grated cheese - a handful

COOKING TIME: 10-15 MINUTES

METHOD

- In a bowl or any type of container you have in a tent or RV combine all ingredients
- Wrap pieces of dough around the stick making sure the dough does not go over one-inch of thickness
- Hold the stick over a campfire for 10 to 15 minutes or until the dough becomes golden brown in color
- Eat warm

Campfire Bacon

INGREDIENTS FOR 2 SERVINGS

- Two strips of bacon (or more if cooking for more people)

COOKING TIME: 5 MINUTES

METHOD

- Wrap bacon around the upper portion of the stick following the one strip for one stick rule (if you plan to cook more bacon, you'll need a stick for each part)
- Cook over a campfire for 5 minutes or until crispy

Cinnamon Rollups

INGREDIENTS FOR 3 SERVINGS

- Crescent rolls – 1 package
- Sugar – ¼ cup
- Cinnamon – 1tbsp

COOKING TIME: 5 MINUTES

METHOD

- In a small bowl or container combine cinnamon and sugar
- Separate crescent rolls and wraps them around the stick and roll into the cinnamon and sugar mixture
- Cook for 5 minutes rotate occasionally

Main Dish

Steak on a Stick

INGREDIENTS FOR 4 SERVINGS

- Steaks – 2
- Salt – 1tbsp
- Black pepper – 1tbsp
- Garlic powder – 1tbsp

COOKING TIME: 15 MINUTES

METHOD

- Combine all seasonings in the same bag and pack with the remaining camping equipment
- Build the campfire
- Season the steaks with seasonings from the bag and take the skewer or a sturdy stick to pierce it through the steak. Ideally, two sticks should go through two edges of the steak because that way the meat won't fall down in the fire
- Cook the steak over the fire for 15 minutes rotating occasionally, or until your preferred doneness

Hot Dogs on a Stick

INGREDIENTS FOR 4 SERVINGS

- Hot dogs – 4 (or as many as you'd like)
- Buns – 4 (the number of buns and hot dogs should be the same)
- Mustard
- Relish
- Onions (diced) – 1 onion (depending on for how many people you're cooking)

COOKING TIME: 5 MINUTES

METHOD

- Gently place a hot dog on a stick
- Use a knife to make diagonal cuts on each dog
- Hold sticks over a campfire for 5 minutes. Rotate occasionally to make sure it is cooked evenly on all sides
- Remove hot dogs from the stick, transfer in the bun, and add mustard, relish, and onions

Side Dish

Campfire Bread on a Stick

INGREDIENTS FOR 8 SERVINGS

- Dried yeast – 1tsp
- Sugar – 1tsp
- Flour – 2 cups
- Olive oil – 2tbsp
- Salt – 1tsp
- Jam to taste

COOKING TIME: 5 MINUTES

METHOD

- First, prepare the dough by mixing all ingredients together in a bowl
- Cover the bowl and let sit in a warm place until it doubles the size (for about an hour). It's a good idea to prepare the dough before setting up a campfire. By the time campfire is steady, your dough will grow
- With floured hands take out the dough and divide it into eight equal pieces
- Stretch each piece of dough into a thin strip and wrap it around a stick. Make sure to

choose sturdy sticks that won't break or drop as you wrap the dough around the top. While wrapping, pinch the dough together to secure the ends if necessary
- Hold the stick over fire rotating to make sure all sides are browned; it usually takes 10 minutes to get your break baked over a campfire
- Add jam and enjoy

Antipasto Stick for RV Campers

INGREDIENTS FOR 12 SERVINGS

- Olives – 12
- Small balls of fresh mozzarella – 12
- Salami – 12 slices
- Pimento-stuffed green olives – 12
- Cherry peppers (halved) – 6
- Pepperoncini peppers – 12

COOKING TIME: 5 MINUTE

METHOD

- Take 12 thin sticks
- Start arranging the ingredients one after another
- Gently pierce through olives, the mozzarella, salami, pimento-stuffed olives, cherry pepper halves, and pepperoncini peppers
- Hold the stick over fire rotating for 5 minutes

Dessert

Shortcake on a Stick

INGREDIENTS FOR 4 SERVINGS

- Baking mix – 2 cups
- Unsalted butter (melted) – 4tbsp
- Heavy cream – ¼ cup
- Strawberries (sweetened to taste) – 2 cups
- Whipped cream

COOKING TIME: 10-15 MINUTES

METHOD

- Start by building a campfire, but let the flames die down
- Combine all ingredients except strawberries and whipped cream in a bowl and mix thoroughly
- Roll the dough into walnut-sized balls, flatten the dough ball and post it on the end of the stick. Wrap the dough around the top of the stick similar to the shape of the corncob
- Hold the stick over the fire for 10 to 15 minutes or until it turns brownish. Make sure

to rotate, so the dough is baked evenly on each side
- Crumble the dough into serving bowl or a plate (depending on the manner of camping whether it's RV or tent) and top with strawberries and whipped cream

Apple Pie on a Stick

INGREDIENTS FOR 4 SERVINGS

- Sugar – 1 cup
- Cinnamon – 1tbsp
- Apples – 4

COOKING TIME: 5-10 MINUTES

METHOD

- Combine sugar and cinnamon in a small container and set aside
- Push the stick through the top of the apple until it is secured i.e., when you're confident it won't fall down
- Roast the apples two to three inches above the fire and turn them frequently so that they are cooked on each side. Bear in mind the skin will start to brown and juice will dribble out as you cook
- Remove apples from the fire when the skin is loose, but don't take out the sticks just yet
- Carefully remove the skin and coat each apple with sugar and cinnamon mixture
- Roast over the fire for a few moments, remove and let cool off

Another option is to dip apples in the sugar/cinnamon mixture and set them aside until they are cool enough to eat.

Chapter 2: Kebab on Skewers

The skewer is a thin wood or metal stick used to hold pieces of food together. They are mainly used to grill meats and fish but have many other applications as well. Basically, you can use skewers to prepare delicious foods with various ingredients. In this chapter, you will see how to make tasty kebab on skewers without too much hassle. The biggest advantage of this cooking method is simplicity. You get to be creative and experiment with ingredients to get a colorful meal. Whether you're camping in a tent or taking your RV, kebab on skewers is a fast, healthy, and delicious cooking method you should definitely try.

Breakfast

French Toast Sausage Kebabs for RV Campers

INGREDIENTS FOR 12 SERVINGS

- Bread slices – 5
- Milk – ¾ cup
- Eggs – 4
- Cinnamon – 1tsp
- Salt – pinch
- Ground pork sausage – 1lb/453g
- Maple syrup – 1/3 cup

COOKING TIME: 10-15 MINUTES

METHOD

- Cut each slice of bread into nine squares
- In a bowl or container, combine milk, eggs, cinnamon, and salt. Whisk thoroughly
- Roll the pork sausage in 24 tight and small balls
- Gently dip bread squares in the egg mixture and take out immediately, then slide them on the skewers followed by sausage, then bread

again. Make sure you do not soak the bread squares because they will be too wet to place on the skewer
- Holdover a campfire for 10 minutes or until bread cubes get the yellow gold color and the meat becomes brownish
- Drizzle kebabs with maple syrup and hold over the fire for an additional 5 minutes

Savory Breakfast Kebabs

INGREDIENTS FOR 6 SERVINGS

- Olive oil – 2tbsp
- Breakfast sausage links (cut into bite-size pieces) – 6
- Onion (cut into chunks) – 1
- Red bell pepper (cut into chunks) – 1
- Green bell pepper (cut into chunks) – 1
- Salt and pepper – to taste

COOKING TIME: 25 MINUTES

METHOD

- Gently place sausage links, onion chunks, and peppers on the skewers
- Drizzle the skewers with olive oil and salt and pepper
- Holdover a campfire for 20 to 25 minutes or until peppers soften

Brown Breakfast Skewers

INGREDIENTS FOR 8 SERVINGS

- Sugar – ¾ cup
- Cinnamon – 3-4 tsp
- Brown and serve rolls (uncooked, quartered) – 8
- Butter (melted) – 1 stick
- Bacon or ham rounds – 1lb/453g

COOKING TIME: 10 MINUTES

METHOD

- Combine sugar and cinnamon in a small container (or a little bowl or even a bag, depending on the camping method)
- Allow butter to melt (put it in direct sunlight) and drizzle it over quartered rolls
- Add sugar mixture and toss to coat
- Thread rolls with ham or bacon on each skewer (you may also add pieces of your favorite seasonal fruit if you can find it in the campsite area)
- Make sure the skewers aren't crowded

- Cook for 10 minutes and serve. You'll have delicious meat and yummy sweet for breakfast on a single skewer

Main Dish

Chicken and Veggie Kebabs

INGREDIENTS FOR 4-6 KEBABS

- Olive oil – ¼ cup
- Basil (chopped) – ¼ cup
- Parsley (chopped) – ¼ cup
- Garlic (minced) – 2 cloves
- Lemon (juiced) – 1
- Salt – 1tsp
- Chicken (boneless, skinless) – ½ lb/226g
- Mushrooms (whole) – 8oz/226g
- Cherry tomatoes – 8oz/226g
- Green onions (cut into 1-inch pieces) – 2-3

COOKING TIME: 10 MINUTES

METHOD

- Combine olive oil, lemon juice, salt, garlic, basil, and parsley in a bigger container or a ziplock bag.
- Add chicken to ingredients in the bag or container and shake for a few seconds to coat thoroughly

- Seal the bag with chicken in it or cover the container for an hour
- In the meantime, fire up the grill or start a campfire
- After the meat has been marinated, build the kebabs by threading the chicken and vegetables on the skewers. Make sure to alternate the ingredients to make skewers colorful
- Holdover fire or grill for 10 minutes

Beef and Onion Skewers

INGREDIENTS FOR 4 SERVINGS

- Steak (cubed) – 1lb/453g
- Coconut aminos – ¼ cup
- Olive oil – 1tbsp
- Lemon juice – 2tbsp
- Green onion (sliced) – 2
- Garlic (minced) – 1 clove
- Red onion (chopped) – 1
- Salt and pepper – to taste

COOKING TIME: 12 MINUTES

METHOD

- In a container or ziplock bag combine all ingredients except steak
- Mix thoroughly and add steak
- Cover the container or seal the bag for one to two hours
- Thread steak cubes ingredients from the ziplock bag or container on the skewers
- Holdover campfire or grill for 10 to 12 minutes occasionally rotating to cook evenly on all sides

Beef Kebab

INGREDIENTS FOR 5 SERVING

- BBQ sauce – ½ cup
- Olive oil – ¼ cup
- Water – ¼ cup
- Lime juice – 2tbsp
- Garlic (minced) – 1tbsp
- Black pepper – ½ tbsp
- Steak – 2lbs/907g
- Whole mushrooms – 1 packaging (fresh)
- Sweet onion – 1
- Cherry tomatoes – a handful
- 15-oz can pineapple chunks – 1
- Zucchini – 2
- Sweet bell pepper – 1

COOKING TIME: 10 MINUTES

METHOD

- Add BBQ sauce, olive oil, water, lime juice, garlic, and black pepper in a container or ziplock bag
- Cut steak into cubes and toss them into the bag or container
- Let marinate for an hour

- Thread skewers with meat followed by mushrooms, onion, tomatoes, pineapple, zucchini, and bell pepper
- Cook over campfire or grill for 5 minutes on each side
- Check meat to see if it's done; if not, put it back on the skewer and cook for a few additional minutes

Vegan Kebabs

INGREDIENTS FOR 6 SERVING

- Firm tofu – 8.8oz/250g
- Green bell pepper – 1
- Red bell pepper – 1
- Tomatoes – 2
- Red onion – 1
- Ground cumin – ½ tsp
- Ground turmeric – ½ tsp
- Soy yogurt – 5.2oz/150g
- Juice from ½ lemon

COOKING TIME: 20 MINUTES

METHOD

- Cut tofu and vegetables into cubes
- Mix dry spices evenly and toss tofu to make sure all chunks are covered
- Start assembling kebabs by alternating ingredients (tofu and vegetables)
- Holdover a campfire for 10 minutes on each side

- Make a sauce using yogurt, lemon juice, and you may also sprinkle some fresh herbs or spices if you bring with you
- Serve kebab alongside the sauce

Smoked Sausage Kebabs

INGREDIENTS FOR 12 SERVINGS

- Smoked sausages – 2 packages
- Red pepper – 1
- Button mushrooms – 1 package
- Yellow squash – 1
- Red onion – 1
- Zucchini – 1

COOKING TIME: 10 MINUTES

METHOD

- Cut sausages into bite-size pieces
- Chop vegetables
- Arrange ingredients on the skewer
- Roast for 10 minutes or until vegetables have a little bit of char on them

Dessert

Marshmallow and Strawberry Kebabs

INGREDIENTS FOR 4 SERVINGS

- Marshmallows – 20
- Strawberries (hulled) – 16

COOKING TIME: 5 MINUTES

METHOD

- Thread four skewers with five marshmallows and four strawberries
- Holdover campfire carefully turning slowly until marshmallows are toasted

Chapter 3: Grate

Are you a fan of barbecue? Who isn't?! Camping is a wonderful opportunity to rest and relax with friends and family. And let's be honest; it's impossible to have a great time without good food. You can have your BBQ meal when camping and grate cooking method can help. The grate is often used on grill surfaces, but for camping purposes, it can replace grill entirely. This way, food is evenly cooked and retains its nutrients for a healthy yet tasty meal. Make sure the food is cooked on a great equal amount of time on each side. These recipes will help you prepare meals in a few minutes only. Before cooking, coat the grate surface with high-heat cooking oil, wipe off excess oil before you heat it. Don't forget to clean the grate thoroughly after use. The best thing about grate cooking method is that it's suitable for both RV and tent camping. Just a grate over fire is enough for people who are camping with tents. If you use an RV grill, then you can also enjoy some restaurant-quality meals made with ease.

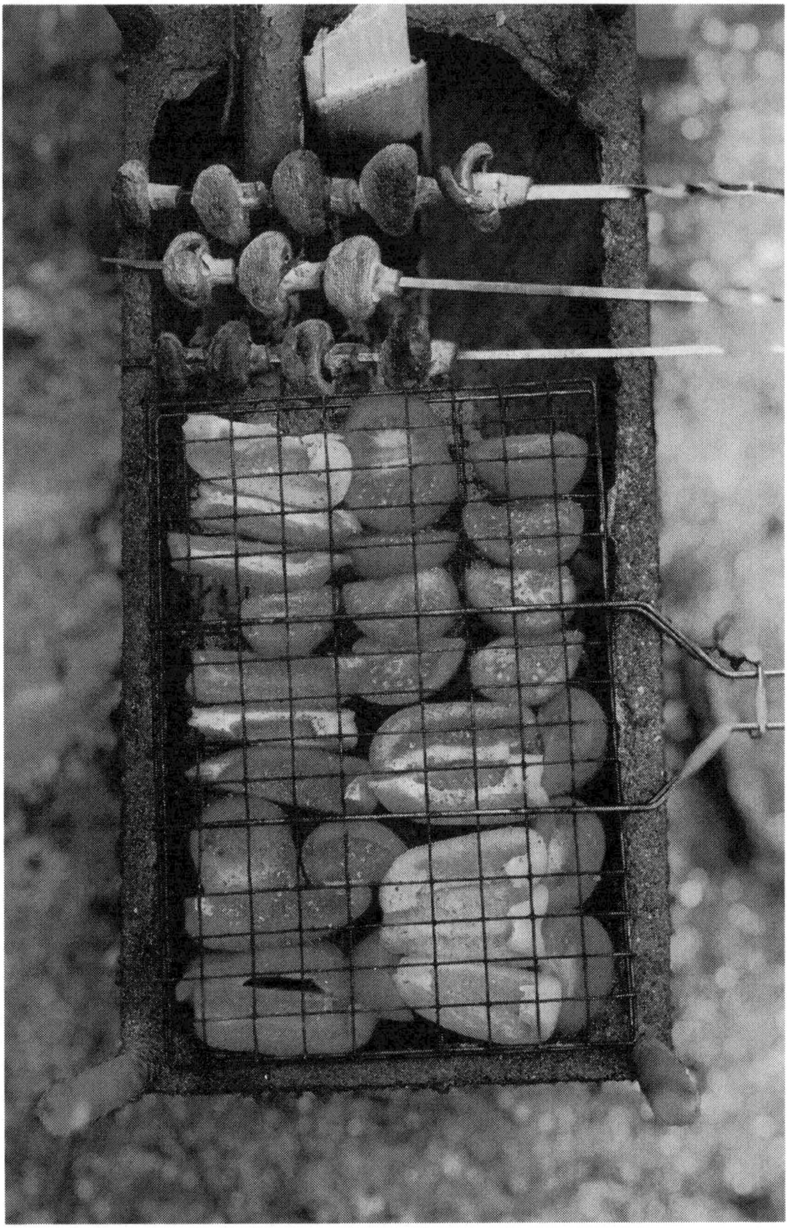

Breakfast

Grilled French Toast

INGREDIENTS FOR 6 SERVINGS

- Bread slices – 6
- Eggs – 6
- Milk – 6oz/1.7dl
- Cinnamon – 1tsp
- Vanilla – 1tsp
- Butter – 6tbsp
- Maple syrup – 1 cup
- Fresh fruit and berries – 2 cups

COOKING TIME: 10 MINUTES

METHOD

- Preheat grill or griddle to medium, or if using the grate only, build campfire underneath
- In a container mix milk, eggs, cinnamon, and vanilla
- Dip each bread piece in the egg mixture for about 20 seconds
- Place bread pieces on the grate and grill for 3 to 5 minutes per side

- Place bread pieces on the grate and grill for 3 to 5 minutes per side
- Garnish with maple syrup and fruit before serving

Cheese Sandwich

INGREDIENTS FOR 4 SERVINGS

- Eggs – 8
- Salt – ¼ tsp
- Pepper – ¼ tsp
- Milk – 1/8 cup
- Butter – 2tbsp
- Cheddar cheese – 8 slices
- Bacon – 12 strips
- White bread – 8 slices

COOKING TIME: 10 MINUTES

METHOD

- Whisk together eggs, milk, salt, and pepper
- In a skillet over grill grate (or grate over a campfire) melt butter, then add egg mixture
- Cook egg mixture three minutes per side
- Grill bacon until cooked
- Transfer egg, bacon strips, and cheese on bread slices to make a sandwich
- Place sandwich on the grate until it turns light brown

Grilled Breakfast Patties

INGREDIENTS FOR 8-10 SERVINGS

(depending on how many patties you make)

- Ground beef – 2lbs
- Salt – 2tsp
- Black pepper – 1 ½ tsp
- Sage (chopped) – 2tsp
- Thyme (chopped) – 2tsp
- Cayenne pepper – ½ tsp
- Red pepper flakes – ½ tsp

COOKING TIME: 10 MINUTES

METHOD

- In a bowl or container add together ground beef, salt, pepper, sage, thyme, cayenne pepper, and red pepper flakes, toss to combine
- Make 8-10 meatballs that you will gently press with your palms to form patties
- Grill patties on a grate for about 5 minutes per side or until they turn brownish in color

Main Dish

Grilled Leg of a Lamb

Cooking time: 1 hour 30 minutes

INGREDIENTS FOR 6-8 SERVINGS

- Leg of lamb (boneless) – 1
- Garlic (minced) – 8 cloves
- Rosemary (minced) – 2tbsp
- Lemon zest – 1tbsp
- Olive oil – 4tbsp
- Salt and pepper – to taste

COOKING TIME: 1 HOUR 30 MINUTES

METHOD

- Coat lamb leg with olive oil, minced garlic, rosemary, and lemon zest
- Season the meat with salt and pepper
- Tie the meat in a butcher twine lightly so it can stay in shape throughout the grilling process, coat with olive oil again and season with salt and pepper

- Place the lamb leg on the grate making sure you preheated the grill or built a steady fire if you're using just a grate over the campfire
- To check the doneness, insert a knife tip at an angle in the middle of the lamb leg. Take out the knife and touch your wrist. If it's cold, the meat is raw. If it's warm or close to body temperature, the meat is medium-rare, and if it's hot, the lamb is well done. Using a meat thermometer, check the temperature. Once it reaches preferred doneness remove the meat from the grate, let it rest, and cover with foil
- 30 minutes before you're ready to have your lunch place the meat back on the grate for a few minutes rotating it occasionally
- Let it rest for 2-3 minutes before you cut the twine
- Slice the lamb leg into pieces of half an inch of thickness and serve

Grilled Salmon

INGREDIENTS FOR 4 SERVINGS

- Salmon fillet (cut into four pieces) -1 lbs/450g
- Olive oil
- Salt and pepper to taste
- Basil (dried) – ¼ cup
- Parsley (dried) – ¼ cup

COOKING TIME: 15 MINUTES

METHOD

- Rub each piece of salmon with olive oil and sprinkle with salt, pepper, basil, and parsley
- Place salmon on the grate and grill five minutes per side, allow it to cook for few more minutes (about five) if your fish is thick
- You'll know salmon is ready when you can easily flake it with a fork
- Serve with vegetables or alone, depending on your personal preferences

Herb Chicken Thighs

INGREDIENTS FOR 5 SERVINGS

- Thyme – 1tbsp
- Oregano – 1tbsp
- Cumin – 1tbsp
- Paprika – 1tbsp
- Salt and pepper – to taste
- Chicken thighs – 10

COOKING TIME: 20-30 MINUTES

METHOD

- Combine all ingredients in a ziplock bag or container and let sit for an hour
- Place chicken thighs on grate and grill for 10 to 15 minutes on each side
- Serve chicken thighs on their own or alongside your favorite sauce or side dish

Grilled Beef-Mushroom Burgers

INGREDIENTS FOR 4 SERVINGS

- Button mushrooms (sliced) – 4oz/113g
- Ground sirloin – 1lb/453g
- Olive oil – 2tbsp
- Salt and pepper – to taste
- Cucumber (chopped) – 1/3 cup
- Greek yogurt – ¼ cup
- Garlic (minced) – 2tbsp
- Lemon juice – 1tbsp
- Lettuce leaves – 8
- Parsley (chopped) – 1tbsp
- Tomato – 4
- Red onion slices – 4

COOKING TIME: 20 MINUTES

METHOD

- Combine very thinly sliced mushrooms with meat, oil, pepper, and salt in a bowl or container and shape into patties
- In a separate bowl or container combine cucumber, yogurt, garlic, lemon juice, parsley, and salt, set aside

- Place burgers on a grate and grill about 4 minutes per side or until your preferred doneness are achieved
- Serve burgers on lettuce leaves and top with yogurt mixture, tomato, and red onion slices

Grilled Chicken and Corn Quesadilla

INGREDIENTS FOR 6 SERVINGS

- Chicken breast (boneless, skinless) – 1lb/453
- Fresh corn – 2 ears
- Cumin – ½ tsp
- Cilantro (chopped) – 2tbsp
- Green onions (sliced) – 2
- Jack cheese (grated) – 1 ½ cups
- Flour tortillas – 6
- Salt and pepper to taste

COOKING TIME: 12 MINUTES

METHOD

- Season chicken breasts with salt
- Grill corn and meat for eight minutes or until chicken is juicy and cooked through, set aside
- When corn cools off a little bit, remove the kernels and dice the chicken
- Combine corn and chicken in a bowl or container with remaining ingredients except for tortillas and whisk thoroughly
- Place ½ cup of the chicken and corn mixture into a tortilla and fold over

- Grill tortillas on a grate for two minutes per side
- Slice and serve

Side Dish

Grilled Wings

INGREDIENTS FOR 6 SERVINGS

- Chicken wings – 48
- Wing sauce of choice
- Ketchup – 4tbsp
- Honey – 2tsp
- Chili powder – 2tsp
- Soy sauce – 3tbsp
- Garlic (pressed or minced) – 2 cloves
- Butter (melted or softened) – 1tbsp
- Spicy mustard – 1tsp
- Red pepper flakes – 1tsp
- Hot sauce – 1-2 tsp

COOKING TIME: 1 HOUR

METHOD

- Season each chicken wing with salt and pepper
- Combine all ingredients from ketchup to hot sauce together to make the glaze
- Glaze every chicken wing generously

- Place chicken wings on a grate for 45 to 60 minutes turning them often for even cooking
- Apply your favorite wing sauce during the last 15 minutes to make sure wings are crispy and have a nice color

Grilled Potatoes

INGREDIENTS FOR 4-6 SERVINGS

- Potatoes (scrubbed) – 4
- Canola oil-2tsp
- Salt and pepper – to taste
- Malt vinegar

COOKING TIME: 25 MINUTES

METHOD

- Cut potatoes into thick slices and coat them with canola oil
- Season potato slices with salt and pepper
- Preheat grill or build campfire upon which you will place the grate
- Place potatoes on the grate for five to seven minutes
- Turn potato slices over and grill for additional 5 to 7 minutes, and repeat the process one more time
- Drizzle with malt vinegar before serving

Dessert

Grate-Grilled Marshmallows

INGREDIENTS FOR 6 SERVINGS

- Graham crackers – 6
- Marshmallows – 6
- Chocolate squares – to taste

COOKING TIME: 10 MINUTES

METHOD

- Spear marshmallow on a stick and hold over grate until it softens and starts to melt
- Place half of a cracker with chocolate on the grate
- As soon as chocolate starts to melt add marshmallow on top
- Place the other half of the cracker on top of the marshmallow and remove the stick
- Repeat the process with remaining crackers and marshmallows

Honey-Rum Grilled Bananas

Cooking time: 15 minutes

INGREDIENTS FOR 4 SERVINGS

- Rum – 2tbsp
- Honey – 2tbsp
- Cinnamon – 1tsp
- Bananas (unpeeled) – 4

COOKING TIME: 15 MINUTES

METHOD

- In a small container combine rum, honey, and cinnamon
- Cut bananas in half, lengthwise, but make sure you don't take their peel off
- Put bananas on the grate cut-side down and grill for three minutes
- Turn bananas and brush with the rum and honey mixture
- Cover and grill for five to six minutes or until bananas are tender
- Peel bananas and serve

Chapter 4: Pie Iron

A pie iron is a cooking appliance consisting of two hinged concave cast iron plates, square or round, on long handles. It's similar to the waffle maker, but without the well-known honeycomb pattern. Pie irons come in multiple shapes and sizes to meet the needs and preferences of different buyers. This is an excellent cooking tool to take camping because it allows campers to prepare food easily and quickly. Campers with tents will appreciate pie iron the most. Steady campfire is all you need to make a tasty lunch. Of course, if you have RV you can use pie iron as well, just make sure to build a fire at a reasonable distance. Before using, preheat pie iron for two minutes before you spray or coat it with oil and fill in with ingredients. Close pie iron, and that's it. In most cases, it takes five minutes to cook a meal, depending on the recipe. In this chapter, you can see some useful pie iron recipes to make on your camping trip.

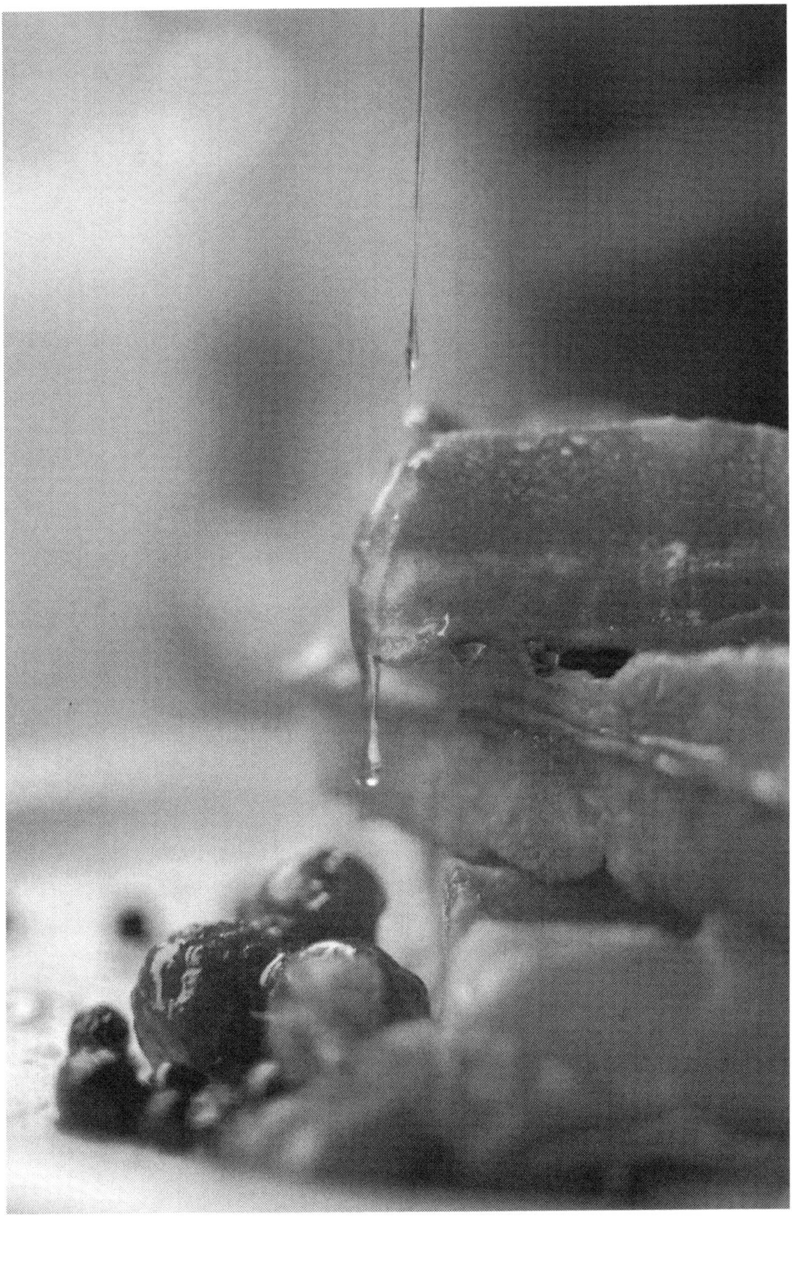

Breakfast

Breakfast Sandwich

INGREDIENTS FOR 1 SERVING

- Bread – 2 slices
- Egg – 1
- Cooked breakfast sausage (crumbled)
- Salt and pepper to taste
- Cheese 1 slice
- Cooking oil spray or butter

COOKING TIME: 2-3 MINUTES

METHOD

- Start by preheating pie iron over a campfire
- Spray or butter both inner surfaces
- Butter one side of the bread slice
- Cut a hole in bread center and place it in the pie iron buttered-side down
- Break an egg directly into the hole and season with salt and pepper
- Top the egg with cheese and cooked sausage and cover the remaining bread slice, and butter it

- Close the pie iron and cook your sandwich for 3 minutes, open to check, flip it over and cook for an additional 2 minutes on the other side.
- You may eat the whole sandwich or cut it in half.
- This recipe is ideal for both RV campers and those who camp in tents

Ham Omelet

INGREDIENTS FOR 4 SERVINGS

- Eggs – 5
- Green pepper (diced) – ½
- Onion (diced) – ½
- Red pepper (diced) – ½
- Cheese (shredded) – ½ cup
- Ham (chopped) – 8oz/226g
- Crescent rolls – 2 packages

COOKING TIME: 6 MINUTES

METHOD

- Scramble five eggs in a skillet over a campfire
- In the meantime, combine green and red pepper, onion, cheese, and ham
- Layout two crescent rolls in the bottom of the pie iron and add egg followed by ham and diced vegetables and cheese, then cover with two crescent rolls
- Close the pie iron and cook over campfire 2-3 minutes per side

Banana Nutella breakfast biscuits

INGREDIENTS FOR 4 SERVINGS

- Canned biscuits – 2
- Hazelnut spread – ½ cup
- Banana – 1

COOKING TIME: 6 MINUTES

METHOD

- Split the biscuits in half
- Press one half on each side of the pie iron
- Add hazelnut spread on biscuits and then place banana slices
- Close the pie iron and cook for 6 minutes rotating occasionally

Main Dish

Super Easy Chicken Pot Pie

INGREDIENTS FOR 1 SERVING

- Grilled chicken breast strips – 6oz/170g
- Mixed vegetables of choice
- Chicken bouillon granules – 1tsp
- Chicken soup – 1 can
- Crescent rolls – 2 tubes
- Salt and pepper to taste

COOKING TIME: 4 MINUTES

METHOD

- In a bowl or container, mix grilled chicken breast strips, chicken bouillon, and vegetables. Season the mixture to taste, set aside
- Place crescent rolls into the pie iron, add chicken mixture, and cover with another crescent roll
- Close the pie iron and cook 2 minutes on each side

- Check whether it's done, if not, allow the pot pie to cook for an additional few minutes if necessary

Monte Cristo

INGREDIENTS FOR 2 SERVINGS

- Eggs – 2
- Salt and pepper to taste
- White bread – 4 slices
- Yellow mustard – 2tbsp
- Mayonnaise – 2tbsp
- Baked ham (sliced) – ½ lb/230g
- Gruyere cheese (shredded) – ½ oz/14g
- Butter – 2tbsp

COOKING TIME: 10 MINUTES

METHOD

- Beat eggs and season them with salt and pepper, set aside
- Make a sandwich with mustard, mayo, ham, cheese, and seasonings according to your personal preferences
- Compress sandwich slightly
- Butter up both sides of the pie iron
- Dip sandwich in beaten egg and place in the pie iron
- Cook 2-3 minutes per side or until brown
- Repeat the process with the second sandwich

Pie Iron Pizza

INGREDIENTS FOR 1 SERVING

- Bread – 2 slices
- Tomato pizza sauce – 2 tbsp
- Pepperoni – based on personal preferences
- Mozzarella cheese – a few slices

COOKING TIME: 5 MINUTES

METHOD

- Place bread slices on both sides of the pie iron
- Add pizza sauce on both bread slices and arrange pepperoni and mozzarella
- Close the pie iron
- Bake for 2 minutes per side

Pie Iron Chicken Pesto Wraps

INGREDIENTS FOR 1 SERVING

- Tortilla – 1
- Pesto – 1tbsp
- Chicken ham - 2-3 slices
- Mozzarella (shredded) – 1/8 cup

COOKING TIME: 6 MINUTES

METHOD

- Put one side of tortilla on pie iron and layer with chicken, cheese, and pesto
- Fold tortilla and close the pie iron
- Cook for 3 minutes per side, but if the fire isn't strong and steady it may take longer

Chicken Chimichangas

INGREDIENTS FOR 4 SERVINGS

- Flour tortillas – 4
- Chicken (cut into pieces) – 1 cup
- Onion (chopped) – ½ cup
- Green pepper (chopped) – ½ cup
- Enchilada sauce – ¼ cup
- Cumin – ¼ tsp
- Salt, pepper, and garlic to taste
- Cheddar cheese (cubed) – ½ cup

COOKING TIME: 10 MINUTES

METHOD

- Combine all ingredients, except tortillas, in a bowl or ziplock bag, whisk thoroughly
- Spoon one to two tablespoons of the mixture into a tortilla and wrap it up
- Butter both sides of pie iron and cook for 10 minutes rotating occasionally or until tortillas get a nice golden color

Dessert

Campfire Fruit Pies

INGREDIENTS FOR 1 SERVING

- Bread slices - 2
- Cinnamon – 1tsp
- Sugar – 1tbsp
- Seasonal fruit – 3tbsp

COOKING TIME: 5 MINUTES

METHOD

- Place a piece of bread on each side of the pie iron
- Put a few tablespoons of fruit on bread and sprinkle with sugar and cinnamon
- Close pie iron and cook for 2-3 minutes per side or until bread slices are golden browns

Peanut Butter Banana Sandwich

INGREDIENTS FOR 1 SERVING

- Banana – 1
- Bread – 2 slices
- Peanut butter – 2tbsp
- Cinnamon - ½ tsp
- Honey – 1tsp

COOKING TIME: 5 MINUTES

METHOD

- Place one bread slice on each side of the pie iron
- Layer peanut butter, cinnamon, honey, and banana on one slice
- Cover the pie iron
- Cook for 5 minutes flipping occasionally or until bread slices are crispy and golden

Chapter 5: Dutch Oven

A Dutch oven is a wide and deep thick-walled cooking pot with a tight-fitting lid. The best thing about Dutch ovens is their versatility i.e.; you can use them to make a wide range of meals, especially soups and stews. Since it's heavy-duty cookware, the Dutch oven is particularly useful for people who are camping in RVs as it's easy to take this pot wherever you go and use it outside. Of course, if you have a tent, you can use it as well, pending you're not walking too much from car to camping spot as its heaviness isn't exactly the most practical piece of gear for long walks. What makes Dutch oven an ideal camping buddy is that it retains heat, and its non-stick nature makes it easy to prepare different meals. At the same time, all ingredients are heated and cooked evenly while retaining their nutritional value. When cooking with a Dutch oven, you need to place it directly over a campfire flame. You can cook with coals from the campfire, but for more precise temperature control, it's practical to use charcoal briquettes. Contrary to popular belief, cleaning a Dutch oven is easy. Wipe out the oven, then fill out with water and bring to a full boil, scrub the interior, rinse with clean water and wipe dry. In this chapter, you're going to see some useful recipes to make on your camping trip.

The table below shows how many coals you need for different temperatures, depending on the size of the Dutch oven.

Temperature	8" (2-4 people)	10" (4-8 people)	12" (8-12 people)	14" (12-16 people)
325°F (162°C)	15 coals (10 top/5 bottom)	19 coals (13 top/6 bottom)	23 coals (16 top/7 bottom)	30 coals (20 top/10 bottom)
350°F (176°C)	16 coals (11 top/5 bottom)	21 coals (14 top/7 bottom)	25 coals (17 top/8 bottom)	32 coals (21 top/11 bottom)
375°F (190°C)	17 coals (11 top/6 bottom)	23 coals (16 top/7 bottom)	27 coals (18 top/9 bottom)	34 coals (22 top/12 bottom)
400°F (204°C)	18 coals (12 top/6 bottom)	25 coals (17 top/8 bottom)	29 coals (19 top/10 bottom)	36 coals (24 top/12 bottom)
425°F (218°C)	19 coals (13 top/6 bottom)	27 coals (18 top/9 bottom)	31 coals (21 top/10 bottom)	38 coals (25 coals/13 bottom)
450°F (232°C)	20 coals (14 top/6 bottom)	29 coals (19 top/10 bottom)	33 coals (22 top/11 bottom)	40 coals (26 top/14 bottom)

Breakfast

Mountain Man Breakfast Casserole

INGREDIENTS FOR 4-6 SERVINGS

- Turkey or pork sausage – 2lbs/907g
- Eggs – 8
- Milk – ¼ cup
- Cheddar cheese – 2 cups
- Potatoes (shredded) – 2lbs/907g
- Salt and pepper to taste

COOKING TIME: 20-25 MINUTES

METHOD

- Start by preheating the 8" Dutch oven to 350°F (176°C) i.e. 11 coals on top and 5 on bottom
- Break up turkey or pork sausage in the oven and fry until it is done
- In the meantime, combine eggs and milk in a separate bowl or container and set aside
- Take cooked meat out of Dutch oven and set aside
- Spread shredded potatoes evenly on the bottom of Dutch oven and lightly brown them,

then layer sausage followed by beaten eggs and grated cheese
- Cover Dutch oven and let cook for 20 to 25 minutes or until eggs are fully cooked

Sausage and Egg Breakfast

INGREDIENTS FOR 4 SERVINGS

- Bell pepper (diced) – 1
- Onion (diced) – 1
- Eggs – 1 ½ dozen(18eggs)
- Sausage – 1lb/453g
- Salt and pepper to taste

COOKING TIME: 5 MINUTES

METHOD

- Cut sausage into bite-sized pieces and brown in an 8" Dutch oven
- Before sausages are completely done, add bell pepper and onion
- Sauté vegetables until onions are translucent
- If there's too much grease from sausages spoon out the excess
- Add eggs and let cook with five coals under and 11 on top, until desired firmness

Breakfast Burritos

INGREDIENTS FOR 8 SERVINGS

- Breakfast sausage – 2lb/907g
- Onions – 2
- Green peppers – 2
- Eggs – 24
- Garlic powder – 2tbsp
- Chili powder – 2tbsp
- Soft tortillas – 16
- Any kind of shredded cheese – 3 cups
- Salsa – 3 cups

COOKING TIME: 10-15 MINUTES

METHOD

- Chop green pepper and onions
- In a 12" Dutch oven fry pepper, sausage, and onion, then remove the mixture from the oven
- Combine garlic, eggs, onion you just fried, and chili powder in Dutch oven until cooked
- Transfer egg mixture to sausage mixture and whisk thoroughly
- Scoop 1/3 cup of mixture on each tortilla then add cheese and roll up

- Lay 5 tortillas in Dutch oven then place other five on top, then add the third layer
- Cover Dutch oven with a lid and bake 10-15 minutes with 6-9 coals underneath it and 12-18 on top of it
- Serve burritos with salsa

French Toast Casserole

INGREDIENTS FOR 6-8 SERVINGS

- French bread – 1 loaf
- Eggs – 8
- Milk – 3 cups
- Sugar – 4tbsp
- Cinnamon – 1tsp
- Salt – ¾ tsp
- Vanilla – 1tsp
- Butter (cut into small pieces) – 4tbsp

COOKING TIME: 30-45 MINUTES

METHOD

- Tear bread in chunks sized about one to two inches and put them in a 10" Dutch oven
- Combine remaining ingredients, except butter and pour them over bread
- Add butter on top
- Place 14 coals on top and 7 on bottom i.e., bake at 350°F (176°C)
- Bake for 30 to 45 minutes or until eggs are set

Whether you camp in an RV or tent, this is an easy and delicious recipe for the most important meal of the day

Family Quiche

INGREDIENTS FOR 6-8 SERVINGS

- Eggs – 12
- Milk – ¼ cup
- Ham, sausage, or bacon (diced) – 1 cup
- Mushrooms (sliced) – 1 cup
- Onion (diced) – 1
- Broccoli – 1 ½ cups
- Grated cheese – 2 cups
- Butter – 2 tbsp
- Salt and pepper to taste

COOKING TIME: 45 MINUTES

METHOD

- Cook meat thoroughly in a 10" Dutch oven, set aside, drain all the grease
- Steam onion, mushrooms, and broccoli for 10 minutes
- Take vegetables out of Dutch oven and set aside
- Wipe out Dutch oven
- In a separate bowl or container combine eggs, salt, pepper, milk, and butter then add meat, cheese, and vegetables

- Add mixture into Dutch oven and bake and cook with 14 coals on top and seven on the bottom for 14 minutes
- Take Dutch oven from the heat but continue baking from the top for additional 20 minutes or until eggs are nicely set

Main Dish

Dutch Oven Nachos

INGREDIENTS FOR 2 SERVINGS

- Oil – 1tbsp
- Tortilla chips – ½ lb/220g
- Hot tomato sauce – 1 can
- Mexican cheese blend (shredded) – 1 cup
- Black beans (drained) – 1 can
- Avocado (cubed) – 1
- Green onions (sliced) – 4-5
- Cilantro (chopped) – a handful
- Lime (wedged) – 1

COOKING TIME: 10 MINUTES

METHOD

- Use oil to lightly coat the bottom of an 8" Dutch oven to make sure nachos don't stick
- Spread 1/3 of tortilla chips at the bottom of the Dutch oven and add ¼ of tomato sauce can be followed by ¼ of black beans, ¼ cup cheese, a handful of avocado, cilantro, green onions. Repeat the same process for the second layer, then the third layer

- Cover the Dutch oven and bake for 10 minutes or until the cheese melts with 10 coals on top and 5 in the bottom.
- Serve nachos with lime wedges

Sprite Chicken

INGREDIENTS FOR 10 SERVINGS

- Uncooked bacon (chopped) – ½ lb/220g
- Boneless chicken (cut into chunks) – 1 ½ lbs/680g
- Red potatoes (cut into bite-sized pieces) – 2 ½ lbs/1100g
- Baby carrots (cut into small pieces) – 1lb/453g
- Onions (sliced) – 2
- Shredded cheese – 1 cup
- Salt and pepper – to taste
- Flour – ½ cup
- Sprite or apple juice – 1 cup

COOKING TIME: 55 MINUTES

METHOD

- Cook bacon pieces in a 12" Dutch oven until they are crispy
- Remove bacon, but leave the grease in the oven
- In a bag combine flour and seasonings, then add chicken and shake to coat evenly

- Brown the chicken in bacon grease and take it out of Dutch oven
- Start adding onions followed by potatoes, carrots, chicken, and bacon in Dutch oven and pour Sprite or apple juice over them
- Place Dutch oven on 11 coals, cover it and place 17 coals on top
- Cook for 45 minutes
- Remove the lid and add cheese, then cover again and cook for 10 minutes

Baked Beans

INGREDIENTS FOR 6 SERVINGS

- Navy beans – 2 cans (or fresh beans)
- Bacon (chopped) – ½ lb/220g
- Onion (chopped) – 1
- Worcestershire sauce – 1tbsp
- Molasses – ¼ cup
- Brown sugar – 4tbsp
- Mustard – 1tbsp
- Ketchup – 2-4tbsp

COOKING TIME: 1-3 HOUR
(depending on the beans used)

METHOD

- In a small container combine Worcestershire sauce, molasses, mustard, ketchup, and brown sugar, stir to combine
- Add beans, onions, and bacon into the mixture and pour into a 10" Dutch oven
- Arrange coals on top of the Dutch oven to maintain the temperature of 350°F (176°C) i.e. 7 coals at the bottom and 14 on top

- Cook for one to 1.5 hours if using canned beans, but if using fresh soaked beans, you may need three hours.

Dutch Oven Macaroni and Cheese

INGREDIENTS FOR 6 SERVINGS

- Milk – 3 cups
- Water – 2 ½ cups
- Salt and pepper – to taste
- Macaroni pasta – 15oz/425g
- Butter – 2tbsp
- Dijon mustard – 1tsp
- Cheddar cheese – 2 cups
- Paprika – a dash
- Tabasco – for serving

COOKING TIME: 15 MINUTES

METHOD

- Combine milk, water, and salt in a 10" Dutch oven and bring to a boil, then add pasta and stir
- Cook pasta for 8-10 minutes with 16 coals on top and 7 at the bottom, then add butter, Dijon, and slowly sprinkle with cheese
- Stir until cheese is melted
- Remove pasta from the heat and season with salt, pepper, and paprika
- Serve with Tabasco sauce

Dessert

Dutch Oven Perry Cobbler Pie

INGREDIENTS FOR 4 SERVINGS

- Strawberries – 2lb/907g
- Blueberries – 12oz/340g
- Blackberries – 12oz/340g
- Sugar – ½ cup
- All-purpose flour – ½ cup
- Lemon juice – 2tbsp
- Lemon zest (grated) – 2tsp
- Buttermilk biscuit dough – 1 tube

COOKING TIME: 1 HOUR

METHOD

- Preheat an 8" Dutch oven to 375°F (190°C), i.e., 11 coals on top and 6 at the bottom
- Combine berries, sugar, flour, lemon zest, and juice in a bowl or container, mix thoroughly and transfer into the Dutch oven
- Separate biscuits and cut them into smaller pieces that you'll arrange on top of mixture in Dutch oven and bake for 30 minutes
- Uncover to check doneness

- Cover and bake for additional 30 minutes until biscuits are baked through entirely

Caramel Apple Cobbler

INGREDIENTS FOR 2-4 SERVINGS

- Apple pie filling – 1 can
- Caramel cake mix – 1 box
- Squeeze margarine – 1 bottle

COOKING TIME: 50 MINUTES

METHOD

- Pour pie filling into an 8" Dutch oven and top with cake mix and margarine
- Bake for 45 to 50 minutes with 11 coals on top and six at the bottom or until the top is bubbly and golden brown

Chapter 6: Cast Iron Skillet

Cast iron skillet has a wide range of applications such as sautéing, pan-frying, baking, searing, broiling, braising, roasting, and other cooking techniques. The versatility of cooking options makes cast iron skillet the ideal piece of equipment every camper should own. This cooking tool allows you to enjoy delicious food instead of relying on readymade meals only.

Yet another reason why cast iron skillet is the perfect camping cookware is the ability to distribute heat evenly along with durability to high temperatures, and it's non-stick. Above all that, the cast iron skillet is a trusted ally for any type of campsite cooking. If you don't need a full-size Dutch oven cast iron skillet is a reasonable choice. Just make sure to clean it properly, and the process is the same as with the Dutch oven. Ideally, you should allow the skillet to heat up a few minutes before you put in ingredients. In this chapter, we are going to focus on different meals you can cook with cast iron skillet when camping.

Breakfast

Campfire Skillet Breakfast

INGREDIENTS FOR 8 SERVINGS

- Bacon (sliced) – ½ lb/226g
- Potatoes (peeled, cubed) – 4 cups
- Onion (chopped) – ½
- Eggs (beaten) – 6
- Cheddar cheese (shredded) – 1 cup

COOKING TIME: 17 MINUTES

METHOD

- In cast-iron skillet cook bacon until it achieves preferred doneness, and set it aside
- In bacon fat in cast iron skillet, add potatoes and onion
- Cook vegetables for 10 to 12 minutes or until softened
- Crumble bacon into onion and potatoes mixture, then add eggs
- Cover cast iron skillet and let cook for 2 minutes or until eggs are set
- Sprinkle cheese on a hot meal before serving

Crustless Quiche

INGREDIENTS FOR 5 SLICES

- Eggs – 10
- Milk – ¼ cup
- Cherry tomatoes (halved) – 6oz/170g
- Mushrooms (sliced) – 4oz/113g
- Spinach (torn) – 2oz/56g
- Thyme (fresh) – 1tbsp
- Cheddar (shredded) – 4oz/113g
- Salt and pepper – to taste
- Butter – 2tbsp
- Red pepper flakes – ½ tsp (optional)

COOKING TIME: 5 MINUTES

METHOD

- In a ziplock bag combine all ingredients except butter, and shake thoroughly to mix
- Melt butter in a cast-iron skillet and pour the egg mixture
- Cover skillet with aluminum foil
- Cook for 3-5 minutes
- Serve immediately

Cast Iron French Toast

INGREDIENTS FOR 4 SERVINGS

- Eggs – 4
- Light cream – ¼ cup
- Vanilla extract – ½ tsp
- Bread – 4 slices
- Vegetable oil – 1 tbsp (divided)
- Butter – 1 tbsp (divided)
- Maple syrup

COOKING TIME: 6 MINUTES

METHOD

- Whisk eggs and combine them with light cream and vanilla
- In a cast-iron skillet heat ½ of oil and ½ of butter
- Dip bread slices in the egg mixture and place them on cast iron skillet
- Cook bread until it becomes golden in color, usually 3 minutes per side
- Take out bread slice, add remainder of oil and butter, and place remaining bread slices dipped in egg mixture
- Serve with maple syrup

Bacon Asparagus Frittata

INGREDIENTS FOR 6 SERVINGS

- Bacon – 12oz/340g
- Fresh asparagus (sliced) – 2 cups
- Onion (chopped) – 1 cup
- Garlic (minced) – 2 cloves
- Eggs (beaten) – 10
- Parsley – ¼ cup
- Salt and pepper to taste
- Tomato (sliced) – 1
- Cheddar cheese (shredded) – 1 cup

COOKING TIME: 25 MINUTES

METHOD

- In cast-iron skillet cook bacon until it's crispy
- Take out bacon, and sauté asparagus, onion, and garlic in bacon grease until onion is soft and translucent
- Crumble bacon and set aside a third of the mixture
- Combine remainder of bacon, parsley, salt, and pepper in a separate bowl or container

- Into cast iron skillet pour egg mixture followed by cheese, tomato, and bacon you've reserved earlier
- Cover the cast iron skillet and cook for 10-15 minutes
- Uncover, and let bake for an additional 2-3 minutes

Main Dish

Hot Mess

INGREDIENTS FOR 6 SERVINGS

- Smoked sausage – 1lb/453g
- Yellow squash – 2
- Tomatoes – 2
- Green bell pepper – 1
- White onion – 1
- Vegetable oil – 2tbsp
- Garlic (minced) – ½ tbsp
- Cajun seasoning – ½ tsp
- Salt and pepper to taste
- Cayenne pepper – ½ tsp

COOKING TIME: 15-20 MINUTES

METHOD

- Cut sausage in half lengthwise and chop into bite-sized pieces, then slice yellow squash and tomatoes
- Chop bell peppers and onion
- Heat oil in cast iron skillet then add garlic and sausage and cook until meat turns brownish

- Gently move sausage to the side of the pan and add green pepper, squash, and onion
- Cook vegetables until they soften and turn brown in color
- Add tomatoes on top and sprinkle with seasonings
- Stir thoroughly and serve

Potatoes with Parmesan

INGREDIENTS FOR 6 SERVINGS

- Olive oil
- Potatoes – 6
- Garlic (minced) – 6 cloves
- Italian seasoning or any seasoning of choice – 1tsp
- Salt and pepper to taste
- Butter (cubed) – ¼ cup
- Parmesan cheese (shredded) – ¼ cup

COOKING TIME: 1 HOUR 30 MINUTES

METHOD

- Coat bottom of cast iron skillet with olive oil and proceed to slice potatoes into thin slices (like chips)
- Arrange potato slices vertically in cast iron skillet and sprinkle with Italian seasoning, garlic, salt, and pepper
- Dot potatoes in a skillet with butter, cover with foil and bake for an hour or until potatoes become soft and tender

- Uncover the skillet and garnish with cheese then keep on fire for 15-20 minutes more, potatoes will be crispy that way

Cast Iron Skillet Vegetables

INGREDIENTS FOR 6 SERVINGS

- Zucchini (sliced) – 1
- Corn on the cob (sliced to thirds) – 1
- Bell peppers (diced) – 2
- Sweet onion (chopped) – 1
- Olive oil – 1tbsp
- Parsley (chopped) – 1tbsp
- Paprika – ½ tbsp.

COOKING TIME: 15 MINUTES

METHOD

- Heat the cast-iron skillet and arrange all vegetables in it
- Drizzle vegetables with olive oil then sprinkle with spices
- Cook for 10-15 minutes or until vegetables soften

Simple Skillet Lunch/Dinner

INGREDIENTS FOR 4 SERVINGS

- Ground beef – 1lb/453g
- Onion (chopped) – 1
- Chili powder – ½ tsp
- Ranch style beans – 1 can

COOKING TIME: 10 MINUTES

METHOD

- Brown ground beef in cast iron skillet together with onion and chili powder
- Pour beans into the skillet and cook until they are heated entirely

Dessert

Berries, Chocolate, and Vanilla Skillet

INGREDIENTS FOR 6 SERVINGS

- Fresh berries – 4 cups
- Sugar – 2tbsp
- Vanilla pound cake (cubed) – 4 cups
- Butter – ¼ cup
- Milk chocolate in pieces (to taste)

COOKING TIME: 10 MINUTES

METHOD

- Combine berries and sugar in a bowl or container and let sit for 10 minutes
- In a large skillet over campfire put butter followed by cubed cake pieces until they turn brown, set aside
- Sprinkle hot cubed cake pieces with chocolate and berries, cover with foil to allow chocolate to melt for 5 minutes

Maple Syrup Pudding Cake

INGREDIENTS FOR 12 SERVINGS

- Butter – 6oz/170g
- Sugar – 1 cup
- Eggs – 2
- Vanilla – ½ tsp
- All-purpose flour – 1 ¾ cup
- Baking powder – 1tsp
- Maple syrup – 1 ½ cups
- Whipping cream – 1 ½ cups
- Salt – pinch

COOKING TIME: 20 MINUTES

METHOD

- Combine butter and sugar in a bowl and gently stir until you get a smooth mixture where you will add eggs, vanilla
- In a different bowl or container combine baking powder and flour and pour them in the egg mixture
- Cover the though and let sit for a few hours
- Coat cast-iron skillet with a butter

- In a saucepan combine maple syrup with heavy cream and bring to a boil, add salt and set aside
- Pour the dough into the skillet and pour maple syrup mixture and bake for 20-25 minutes or until the pudding becomes golden brown
- Let cool for 5 minutes before serving

Chapter 7: Foil Packets

As you can conclude by the name, foil packets refer to a method of preparing food in a foil. Perfect for people who camp with tents, foil packets are also useful for RV campers who don't want to spend a lot of time prepping and cleaning up after cooking. The process is simple; combine ingredients in a foil, wrap carefully, and place on the campfire. The best thing about foil packets is that everyone can handle this cooking method; no culinary experience is required. So, if you're looking for a convenient way to eat a delicious meal at the campsite that doesn't involve bring pots or skillets, then foil packets are an obvious choice. Options as to meals you can make are endless, but in this chapter, we are going to focus on the most interesting recipes you can try.

Breakfast

Egg Bake Breakfast

INGREDIENTS FOR 4 SERVINGS

- Cheddar cheese (shredded) – 1 ½ cup (divided)
- Ham (diced) – 1 cup
- Salt – ½ tsp
- Pepper – ¼ tsp
- Eggs – 6
- Milk – ½ cup

COOKING TIME: 5-6 MINUTES

METHOD

- In a container combine eggs, milk, salt, and pepper, then add diced ham and ¾ cup cheese
- Divide mixture among four pieces of nonstick foil and fold and seal tightly
- Place foil packets over the grill grate or campfire for 5-6 minutes or until the eggs are cooked through
- Sprinkle the breakfast with the remainder of cheddar cheese before serving

Foil Packet French Toast

INGREDIENTS FOR 6 SERVINGS

- Eggs – 2
- Milk – 1 cup
- Sugar – 1tbsp
- Bread slices – 6
- Cinnamon – ½ tsp
- Walnuts (crushed) – 4tbsp
- Strawberries – 6
- Lemon (juiced) – ½
- Mint leaves for garnish

COOKING TIME: 5-6 MINUTES

METHOD

- Using a foil create a packet where you will place the bread slice
- In a bowl combine eggs, milk, sugar, and cinnamon
- Pour the mixture over bread slice in the foil packet and top it with walnuts, strawberries, and a little bit more cinnamon
- Soil the foil packet and cook until toast is crispy

- Before serving sprinkle with lemon juice and mint leaves

Sandwich Loaf with Ham and Cheese

INGREDIENTS FOR 6 SERVINGS

- Bread – 1 loaf
- Butter or margarine (softened) – 3tbsp
- Mustard – 1tbsp
- Swiss cheese – 6 slices
- Ham (sliced) – ¾ lb/340g

COOKING TIME: 15 MINUTES

METHOD

- Slice bread, but without cutting it all the way to the bottom. Take butter and keep it in the sun so it can soften
- Stir together mustard and butter
- Spread every other slice of bread with about 2 teaspoons of mustard mixture, so it can make a total of 6 sandwiches
- Fold each slice of Swiss cheese diagonally and tuck into a sandwich
- Tuck ham into a sandwich loaf as well

- Place the loaf on the foil making sure it is covered on all sides
- Cook over grill or campfire for 15 minutes or until cheese is melted and bread hot. Make sure to rotate the loaf frequently while it's cooking
- Pull apart sandwiches before serving

Main Dish

Indian Spiced Baked Potato in Foil

INGREDIENTS FOR 6 SERVINGS

- Golden yellow potatoes (sliced) – 4 cups
- Olive oil – 3-4tbsp
- Smoked paprika – ½ tsp
- Garlic (minced) – ½ tsp
- Curry powder – ½ tsp
- Salt and pepper to taste
- Eggs – 4

COOKING TIME: 30 MINUTES

METHOD

- Combine potatoes and seasonings
- Place potatoes in a packet made of foil
- Place foil packets over the campfire and cook for 25 to 30 minutes rotating occasionally
- Open the foil and pour beaten eggs, close it again, and cook for an additional few minutes
- Remove from fire and garnish with extra spices or seasonings if needed

Country Potatoes

INGREDIENTS FOR 4 SERVINGS

- Yellow potatoes (thinly sliced) – 4
- Onion (sliced) – 1
- Garlic (chopped) – 1 clove
- Butter – 4tbsp
- Basil – 1tsp
- Oregano – 1tsp
- Salt and pepper to taste

COOKING TIME: 35 MINUTES

METHOD

- Start by placing 2 tablespoons of butter on the center of the foil then arrange potatoes, garlic, and onion
- Sprinkle potatoes with seasonings and add remaining 2 tablespoons of butter on top
- Carefully close foil by bringing ends of top layer together and cook over a campfire for 30 to 35 minutes
- Serve directly from the foil

Shrimpy Steak Foil Packet

INGREDIENTS FOR 4 SERVINGS

- Sirloin steak (cubed) – ½ lb/226g
- Shrimp (cleaned, deveined) – ½ lb/226g
- Corn – 2 ears (divided into four pieces)
- Red onion (sliced) – 1
- Cherry tomatoes – 1 cup
- Lemon (wedged) – 1
- Garlic (sliced) – 2 cloves
- Olive oil – 4tbsp
- Thyme – 4 sprigs
- Salt and pepper – to taste
- Parsley (chopped) – 1 tbsp

COOKING TIME: 16 MINUTES

METHOD

- Prepare 4 foil packets where you will evenly distribute steak, shrimp, corn, red onion, tomatoes, lemon wedges, and garlic
- Season with thyme, salt, and pepper, drizzle with olive oil
- Fold the foil paper and cook over campfire or grate for 6 to 8 minutes per side
- Before serving sprinkle with parsley

Foil Packaged Chicken Breast

INGREDIENTS FOR 4 SERVINGS

- Chicken breast (boneless, skinless, cubed) – 1lb/453g
- Onions (diced) – 2
- Fresh mushrooms (sliced) – 8oz/226g
- Yellow bell pepper (sliced) – 1
- Red bell pepper (sliced) – 1
- Garlic (sliced) – 4 cloves
- Potatoes (cubed) – 4
- Olive oil – ¼ cup
- Lemon (juiced) – 1

COOKING TIME: 40 MINUTES

METHOD

- In a ziplock bag or a bowl, combine chicken breast with onion, mushrooms, bell peppers, potatoes, and garlic, sprinkle with olive oil and lemon. Whisk to combine
- Divide the mixture evenly between four aluminum foil packets and cover each packet with a foil as well
- Cook for 40 minutes over a campfire or until potatoes are tender and chick opaque

Lemon Garlic Foil Packet

INGREDIENTS FOR 4 SERVINGS

- Raw shrimp (peeled, deveined) – 1lb/453g
- Butter – 4tbsp
- Garlic (minced) – 3 cloves
- Lemon zest – 1tsp
- Lemon juice – 1tbsp
- Parsley (dried) – 1tsp
- Red pepper flakes – ¼ tsp
- Salt and pepper to taste

COOKING TIME: 15 MINUTES

METHOD

- Place the shrimp in the center of foil packet then add butter and the rest ingredients
- Fold the foil and cook over a campfire for 8-10 minutes, then flip the packet and continue cooking for 3-5 minutes
- Serve on its own or in combination with a side dish of your choice

Jambalaya Foil Packet

INGREDIENTS FOR 5 SERVINGS

- Sausage (sliced) – 1lb/453g
- Yellow onion (diced) – ½
- Red bell pepper (diced) – 1
- Green pepper (diced) – 1
- Celery (diced) – 2 ribs
- Cajun seasonings – 3tsp
- Instant rice – 1 cup
- Water/Chicken broth – 1 cup

COOKING TIME: 25 MINUTES

METHOD

- In a large bowl or container combine all ingredients
- Divide the mixture between 4 foil packets
- Place over the campfire and cook 20-25 minutes or until rice softens

Bacon Ranch Chicken Packet

INGREDIENTS FOR 5 SERVINGS

- Butter (melted) – 6tbsp
- Ranch seasoning powder – 2tbsp
- Salt and pepper to taste
- Chicken breasts – 4
- Red potatoes (quartered or halved) – 1lb/453g
- Cheddar cheese (shredded) – 1 cup
- Bacon (cooked and crumbled) – 4 slices
- Parsley (chopped) – 2tbsp

COOKING TIME: 45 MINUTES

METHOD

- In a small container or bowl combine butter, ranch seasoning, salt and pepper, and whisk thoroughly
- Drizzle potatoes in a bowl with ranch butter mixture and toss to coat evenly
- Place a chicken breast into each foil packet and season with salt and pepper
- Distribute potatoes evenly among foil packets
- Fold the edges and cook over a campfire for 30 minutes

- Sprinkle cooked ingredients with cheese and bake for a few additional minutes
- Before serving make sure to sprinkle with bacon and parsley

Easy Baked Fish in Foil Packets

INGREDIENTS FOR 2 SERVINGS

- Whitefish fillets – 2
- Olive oil – 1tbsp
- Chives (chopped) – 2tbsp
- Potato (diced) – 1 cup
- Vegetables of your choice (chopped) – 2 cups
- Thyme – 2tsp
- Lemon – 1
- Salt and pepper to taste

NOTE: the most practical thing to do is to choose seasonal vegetables for this foil packet.

COOKING TIME: 25 MINUTES

METHOD

- Prepare 2 separate foil packets
- In a bowl, container or Ziploc bag combine olive oil, herbs, and vegetables and mix well
- Drizzle the foil with a little bit of olive oil
- Distribute vegetables evenly between 2 foil packets
- Arrange one fish fillet on top of vegetables in each foil packet
- Sprinkle with lemon juice

- Bring two ends of foil together to close the packet and place over the campfire where you will bake fish and vegetables for 25 minutes or until fish is fully cooked through
- Serve straight in the foil and enjoy

Dessert

Banana Marshmallow in Foil Packet

INGREDIENTS FOR 1 SERVING

- Bananas (peeled)
- Miniature marshmallows
- Peanut butter
- Chocolate chips
- Graham crackers

NOTE: the amount of ingredients depends on the number of bananas and your personal preferences

COOKING TIME: 5 MINUTES

METHOD

- Halve banana lengthwise and place on aluminum foil with the flat side up
- Coat flat side of banana with peanut butter and sprinkle with chocolate chips and marshmallows
- Wrap up foil securely and cook for 5-6 minutes or until marshmallows become slightly toasted
- Remove from fire and sprinkle with crackers

Chapter 8: Camping Shopping List

In order to make your camping trip memorable, it's crucial to make proper plans and pack everything you'll need. Below, you can see the list of things you may want to take camping with you.

- Tent
- Sleeping bags
- Headlamps or flashlights
- Camp chairs
- Lantern
- Extra cord
- Firestarter/matches
- Cook pots
- Potholder
- Dutch oven
- Eating utensils
- Sharp knife
- Bottle opener/can opener/corkscrew
- Cups
- Camp grill
- Grill rack/grate
- Charcoal

- Portable tea/coffee maker
- Sunscreen
- Insect repellent
- First-aid kit

When it comes to food itself, it's good to plan your meals immediately before you go camping. Create a list of ingredients and buy what's necessary to make delicious meals.

Conclusion

Thank you for reading this cookbook. Hopefully, this book motivated you to cook on the next camping trip instead of eating readymade meals. Camping cooking is fun, easy, and a much better way to improve the overall experience. This cookbook featured a multitude of recipes that you can easily make, even if you're not a pro chef.

Next time you go on a camping trip, try to make some of your favorite meals from this Camping Cookbook. You and your friends or family will love it, for sure.

Remember, camping cooking is all about preparing unbelievably delicious foods without too many ingredients. And, if you've wanted to use a cookbook without hard-to-find ingredients, this is the ideal solution; the Camping Cookbook uses only accessible and simple things that make the whole process effortless and relaxing.

In the end, if you liked Camping Cookbook, make sure to review and rate it. Your feedback would be much appreciated.

Thank you.

Written by: Sam Anderson
Copyright©2020
All rights reserved.

All Rights Reserved. No part of this publication or the information in it may be quoted from or reproduced in any form by means such as printing, scanning, photocopying or otherwise without prior written permission of the copyright holder.

Disclaimer and Terms of Use: Effort has been made to ensure that the information in this book is accurate and complete, however, the author and the publisher do not warrant the accuracy of the information, text, and graphics contained within the book due to the rapidly changing nature of science, research, known and unknown facts, and internet. The Author and the publisher do not hold any responsibility for errors, omissions or contrary interpretation of the subject matter herein. This book is presented solely for motivational and informational purposes only.

Made in the USA
Columbia, SC
09 March 2023